INTERACTIVE
DAY TRADING

Sell
Buy

Satish Gaire

ISBN-13: 978-1-951403-06-5 (Paperback)
ISBN-13: 978-1-951403-07-2 (eBook)

The authors disclaim responsibility for adverse effects or consequences from the misapplication or injudicious use of the information contained in this book. Mention of resources and associations does not imply an endorsement.

Co-Authored *by* Nikesh Chapagain
Book Interior *by* Pankaj Runthala

First Edition

"Stock Market is a vehicle that can have astounding impact on your life, Let's make that a *positive* one."

Labor Omnia Vincit

Resources

Unlock Extra Tools & Resources

TradingUniversity.io

This course **includes video modules** that you can access from

DayTradingBook.net

Video Module

Disclaimer

The author and EvilTrader.net ("the company"), including its employees, contractors, shareholders and affiliates, is NOT investment advisory service. We are not registered as a securities broker-dealer or an investment adviser either with the U.S. Securities and Exchange Commission (the "SEC") or with any state securities regulatory authority. We are neither licensed nor qualified to provide investment advice. To the fullest extent of the law, we will not be liable to any person or entity for the quality, accuracy, completeness, reliability, or timeliness of the information provided in the report, or for any direct, indirect, consequential, incidental, special or punitive damages that may arise out of the use of information we provide to any person or entity (including, but not limited to, lost profits, loss of opportunities, trading losses, and damages that may result from any inaccuracy or incompleteness of this information). Every trade you make is your own trade and you are fully responsible for any gain or loss you shall incur. EvilTrader.net, nor any moderators are held liable for any losses you shall have at any time you are with our service or after. It should be not be assumed that the methods, techniques or indicators provided in the book will be profitable nor that they will not result in loss. All information is provided for educational purpose only. Investors and traders must always consult with their licensed advisors or tax advisors to determine the suitability of any investment. We are not liable for any consequences that may occur by using information on this book.

How This Book Works

Welcome To DayTrading Book! *As you can notice,* this book is a little different than any other book that you have read, it's because, **I only have one desire:** *I want you to learn.* I have no interest in making this book thick and filling it with nonsense about my life that's no use to you.

Most stock books get it wrong. They give you pages and pages of information, but there's no advice. A good book doesn't give you information, it gives you specific actionable advice. This is what this book was designed to do.

So, How do you use this book?

Read each chapter individually in the order.

For each chapter:

Step 1: Read the chapter text
Step 2: Watch the Video By Scanning QR Code (Don't skip this)
Step 3. Take the mini quiz (This will reinforce knowledge)

Your task now is to just learn these chapters individually, they all come together at the end and you can use it as a collective strategy.

After reading this book: You should be one of the most knowledgeable people in your circle about stocks.

Companion Video Modules

This Book Includes Interactive **Video Modules & Quizzes** to help you master each of the topics. You can access the video modules by **scanning the QR Code** or **registering an account** at DayTradingBook.net

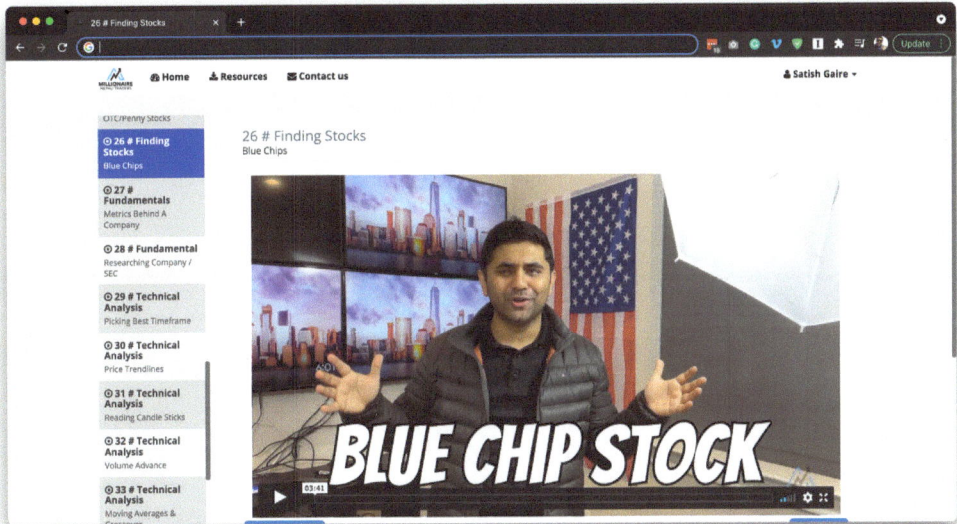

DayTradingBook.net

Seriously, Don't Fool Around

Do you know what type of people I hate?

People who spend money on books and never read them.

The stock market is one of the **GREATEST Inventions of our lifetime**. It's a vehicle that *doesn't judge*. It can give you riches beyond your imagination or put you to the ground.

That's why, while reading each chapter: *I want you to pay attention. This book could be the turning point in your life that turns your life around.*

> *Let's make a pledge:*
>
> *I, _____, promise to read this book with an open*
>
> *mind, give it my full attention because my future could depend on it.*
>
>
> _____ (Sign Here)

Table of Contents

Getting Started

Technical Analysis

Trading Using Indicators

Company Fundamentals

Finding Stocks To Play

Psychology

Putting it all Together

Advance

Getting Started

In the following Chapters, We will learn the foundation to getting started in trading and learn some groundwork. Foundations could be boring but they are SUPER important.

1 Funds and Type of Trader

How much money to start off with?

Money is the least of your priority at this point. (really!) If you give $1M to someone who has no idea how to trade, he will bankrupt himself.

Here's my suggestion: **Teenager:** Start with $100 **College Student:** $500-$1,000 **Adult:** $1,000+

Even if you have the funds, please for gods' sake, do not put it all on your brokerage.

There are 3 types of traders.

1. **Day Trader:** Buys and sells the same security "stock" on the same trading day. Daytraders are capitalizing on the fluctuation that happens in a certain timeframe.

2. **Swing Trader:** Buys a security today and sells it in another trading day. This trader is expecting good news such as "earnings" or press releases.

3. **Investor:** Buys to hold for more than 6 months. Day-to-day fluctuation doesn't matter to him.

Video Module

Can you do all of them at the same time? *Yes*, I encourage you to do so. (and I will teach you all of this)

2 7 Mistakes New Traders Make

Read these & Read them again for lunch & dinner & do not make these stupid mistakes!

If you can just follow these 7 things, you will not lose money. Remember, Stock market strategies are about staying consistent with your PRINCIPALS!

- ☠ Don't trade based on what your friends are hyping up on FB/IG.
- ☠ Not doing research on the company. (Have no idea what the company sells)
- ☠ Too much confidence " Beginners luck does not mean you are smart"
- ☠ The market doesn't care about your feelings
- ☠ Too many positions at once
- ☠ Don't buy on early pre-market (At least when you are starting)
- ☠ No Revenge trading

Video Module

3 Which Brokerage To Use

All Brokers have their own PROS and CONS, but it's best to start with something that's easy to use so you can get the feel for it & later upgrade as you get more experienced.

Recommendation:

Early starting out: Robinhood

Super easy to use & their user interface is built for beginners and everyday traders who do not have prior experince. Their execution time is not the greatest.

After 3-4 months: WeBull

WeBull is a mix between Robinhood and TD. They have all the cool graphics without the hassle and gets the job done.

After 6 Months: TDAmeritrade/ThinkOrSwim

ThinkOrSwim is really advanced. It will be really confusing at the beginning but it has features and tools that none of the other platforms have. This is ideal after you get used to the markets and have some experince.

Video Module

If these are none of your options, please scan the QR Code & we will have suggestions for you.

Cash account is pretty much all the money you transferred from your bank. **Margin account** lets you *"loan"* money from the brokerage, so you can leverage more money.

Margin Account

Can use margin to buy more shares than cash account

Can short sell stocks

Subject to PDT rule

Can lose more money than is in account

Subject to margin call

Must have $25,000 to day trade if labeled as Pattern Day Trader

Pattern Day Trader are eligible for day trading buying power (4X BP)

Subject to interest charge on shares hold overnight on margin

VS

Cash Account

Can only trade with available cash in account to buy stock

Cannot short sell stocks

Subject to free riding rules

Can only lose the cash you are trading with

Subject to cash settlement

There is an advantage to a margin account: You do not have to wait for money to settle before reusing it. *For example:* You bought $100 worth of stock, and sold it for $200. You can instantly use $200 to buy something else right away. On Cash account, you would have to wait 2-3 days to use that $200.

There is also a "con": While I recommend you get a margin account, being able to spend more money than you can have Fear of missing out "FOMO" effect and you might buy something just because you can while that transaction could go wrong.

My Recommendation: I want you to be a responsible adult. Get a margin account and don't be stupid.

Video Module

5 Paper Trading

Paper Trading is when you play with fake money to buy/sell. While I strongly recommend you to use paper trading to learn how the trading software works. *Paper trading will not have the same emotions as trading with real money.* Think about it for a second, it's super easy to spend $1M of fake money to buy Apple stocks. Your brain will not attempt to think it out because it knows there won't be consequences.

Use paper trading to learn how your trading software works.

Learn these key things:

- How to enter a trade
- How to exit a trade
- How to look at a graph

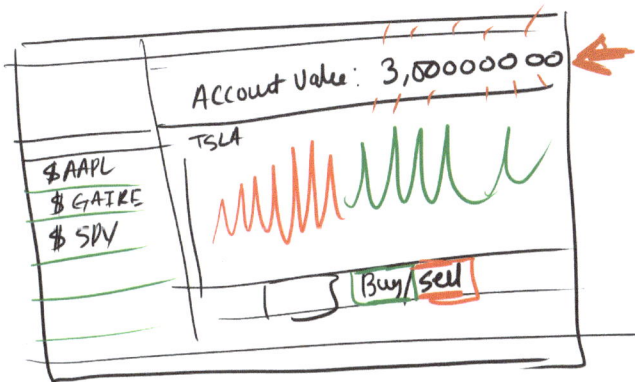

(Don't skip the video lesson)

Video Module

6 PDT and How to AVOID it (3 ways)

PDT is **Pattern day trading**, it only applies to traders in the United States, It doesn't apply to other countries. PDT rule says that you must have 25$k account value on your account a day before in order for you to do unlimited day trading.

Day trading refers **to buying then selling or selling short then buying the same security on the same day**. Just purchasing a security, without selling it later that same day, would not be considered a day trade.

If you have less than $25k, you can ONLY do 3-day traders in 5 trading days. 4th-day trade could lock your account for 90 days.

How do you avoid it:

- **Cash Only Account:** Cash accounts are exempt from PDT rule.
- **Have 3 brokerage account:** Play the system
- **Use it as a limiting factor:** You do not need to day trade every day!

😀 **PRO TIP:** If you account does get flagged, Call your broker and ask to remove the limitations. Some brokers let you do this once a year!

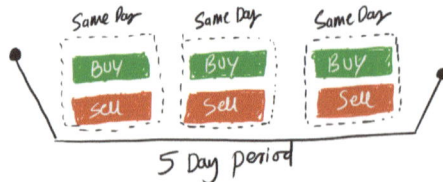

Video Module

7 Platform and useful Indicators

Regardless of what broker you use to trade, we will use a technical platform to do our research and technical analysis. The best platform on market currently is TradingView.

Go to TradingView.com and create a free account & watch the video lesson by scanning the QR code.

Useful Indicators

- **SMA** - Simple Moving Average
- **RSI** - Relative Strength Index
- **MacD** - Moving Average Convergence / Divergence

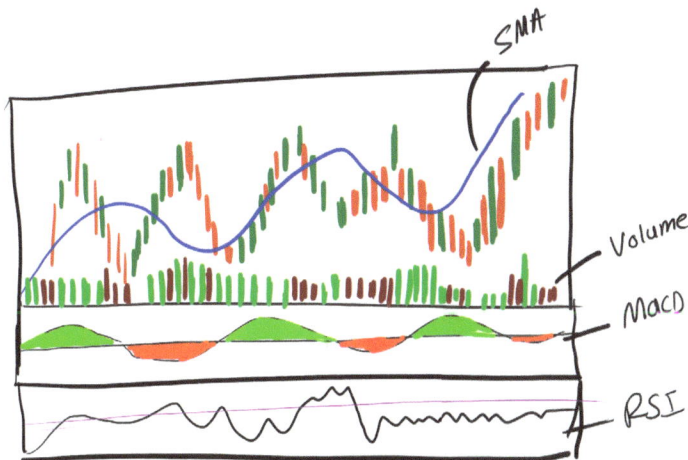

8 Risk Management and Position Sizing

Ever buy a stock and it goes 50% down the minute after you buy it?

- **Not anymore!**

Position Sizing: If you are going to buy $100 worth of stock, then instead of spending the entire $100 at once, you split it in a different percentage size.

- 50% first then 25% and Last 25% At a certain timeframe. (1 min, 5 min, 15 min)

Why do we do this?

- Lower Cost Average & Security

What if the stock keeps going up? You still buy what you intended.

Do we also use the same method to sell security? If there is uncertainty that it could go higher, yes. You sell in sizes.

Video Module

Types of Orders

9

Everytime you place an "order" to buy/sell a security you have to choose an order type, *typically, the default will be "Market Order"*, which is good for the brokerage to make extra few pennies but not so good for you because you don't know what price it will execute at.

Therefore, It's important to use **LIMIT ORDER** when buying and selling a stock.

Order Type	Market Order	Limit Order	Stop-Loss Order	Stop-Loss Limit Order
Definition	Buy/sell at best available price	Buy/sell at a specified price or better	Buy/sell when price reaches a specified point	Limit order activated at a predetermined price
Price control	None	Full control	Once stop price is triggered, no control	Full control

In video module:

- Learn about all order types
- When to use Market order
- Other types of orders

Video Module

Long VS Short Selling

Ever gone to a bar and someone asks you *"Are you long or short Tesla?"* What they are asking is, *do you think Tesla will go up or down?* If you think Tesla will go up, you say, *"I am long Tesla" and if you think,* it will go down, you say *"I am short Tesla"*

In most of the trades you do, you will be "long", you want to BUY LOW and SELL HIGH (🐻) but if you are short-selling, you "borrow" the stock from your brokerage at it's peak (hopefully) , sell it to the market, then buy it back from market when the price goes down, and return the lent stock back to the broker, you keep the difference.

For example, you "borrow" or Short $TSLA when it's at $1,000 & sell it in market and when price goes down to $900, you buy it from market to "CLOSE" the position, you profit $100. You can make money from shorting stocks, but it puts you at UNLIMITED RISK. What if $TSLA goes to $2,000? or $10,000? You have to buy it back & to close the position.

For now, Don't short sell. Just focus on "LONG". I just wanted you know know what short selling is.

Ideal outcome for short sellers

Original share price ↓   Price falls

Make profit

Bad outcome for short sellers

Original share price ↓   Price rises

Make a loss

In The Video Module:

- Long Vs Short
- Short Selling

Video Module

3 Things to check Everyday

If you want to succeed in stock, you need to check 3 things every day.

1. **News:** Always know what's happening with the security that you own, know what is rumor and what is actual news. Always BUY GOOD rumors and sell the news. (Yahoo News, Benzinga.com)

2. **Futures:** Futures indices indicate how the market might perform later in the day or later in the hour. You should not fight the market, you should go with the market. (Investing.com, CNBC.com)

3. **Economic Calendar:** These are special dates set by the reserve bank, on these days, do not trade until the economic news has come out.

Let's watch the video & I will show you how to look at these how to interpret these.

Stock Sectors

Stock industries are vital to understanding how a specific stock will perform. For example, Let's say that Bank Of America is not doing to great but the entire Banking Industry is, that means that once the issue/news settles the stock will catch up to it's industry avg gain/loss.

You should also know which sector each stock falls in. ie. Oil & Gas, Energy, Tech etc

In the video:

- Looking at sectors
- Sector vs Specific company correlation
- Choosing where to invest

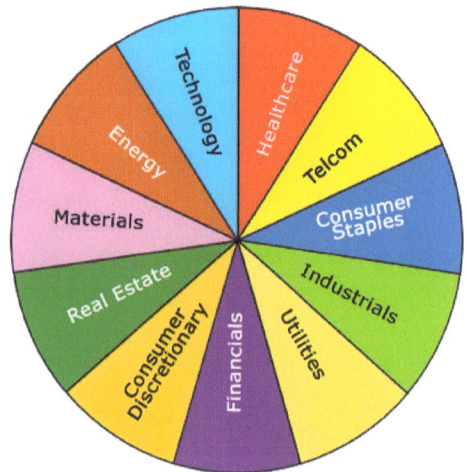

Video Module

Watchlist and Scanner

Watchlists and scanners are the foundation to finding stocks. You might wonder how are people finding good stocks to trade, they know how to effectively use a watchlist and scanner.

This chapter is going to be one of those " enlightening" moments in your life.

Watchlist: Categorized list of stocks that you want to keep an eye on.
Scanner: Scanning for stocks based on various variables

In the video:

- Creating a watchlist
- How to scan for stocks

Video Module

14 Do Something Amazing

Question for you:

If you could do something really nice for a person that you will never meet, would you do it?

Right Now, Go to the site where you purchased this book: Amazon, Walmart, Barnes & Noble etc & leave an honest review about what you think about this book.

This feedback will help someone that you will never ever meet. Because of you, they might pick up this book & make an impact in their life.

Please take a moment to review this book on AMAZON.

Technical Analysis

Now, we will learn important concepts of Technical Analysis. These chapters will help you understand that 99% of traders don't.

15 Time Frame: The Important Of All

When you are looking at a stock price chart, you always have to know what time frame you are looking at. **Timeframe** changes the way your graph looks, therefore it's super important to check the timeframe before making a decision.

Pick the timeframe that MATCHES Duration Of Your Position

Reference:

1-20 minutes: DayTrading, Detailed, Fast-Paced

Daily/Weekly: Swing, Relaxed

Monthly: Long term trades/ trends, low details high confidence

5 minutes

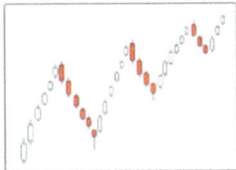

30 minutes

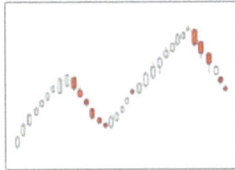

Daily

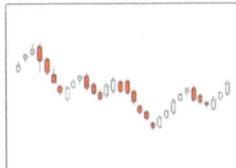

Monthly

In the video:

- Looking at various time frames
- Changing time frames
- TradingView Timeframe

Video Module

Volume tells you if the market is *"liquid"*, meaning, is there money changing hands? If you buy a stock that has super low volume, then you might not be able to sell your stock.

You won't have to worry about volume too much, but you could be looking at a stock that's doing really well, but you have never heard of this company, you want to make sure that you can exit later once you have made money. That's why volume is important

In the video:

- Looking at different volumes
- Volume Patterns

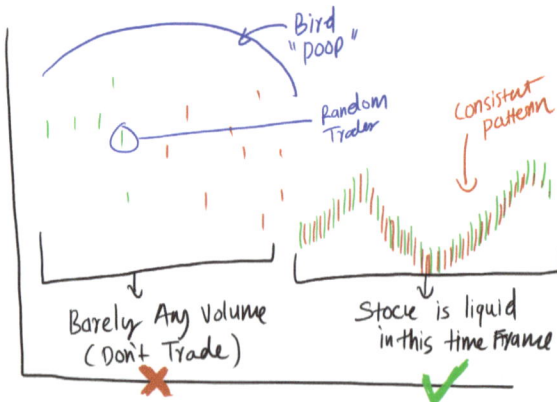

Video Module

A **candlestick chart** is a style of financial chart used to describe price movements of a security, derivative, or currency. It is similar to a bar chart in that each candlestick represents all four important pieces of information for that day: open and close in the thick body; high and low in the "candle wick"

In the video we will learn:

- Why candlesticks vs other charts?
- How to read candlesticks
- How to draw candlesticks
- Important concepts

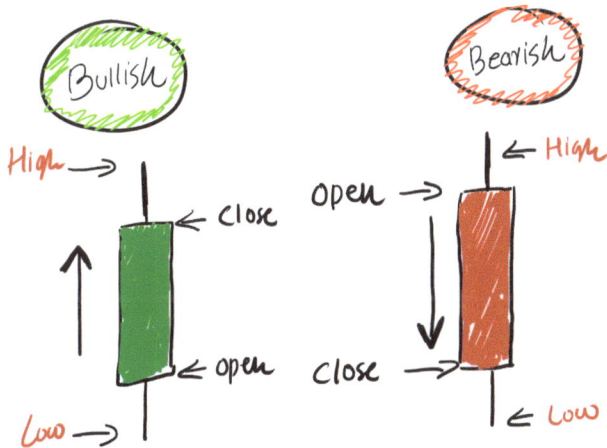

Video Module

PRICE DECREASED / **PRICE DECREASED**

OPEN — HIGH — CLOSE
CLOSE — LOW — OPEN

HIGH = CLOSE / HIGH = OPEN

LOW = OPEN / LOW = CLOSE

OPEN = CLOSE

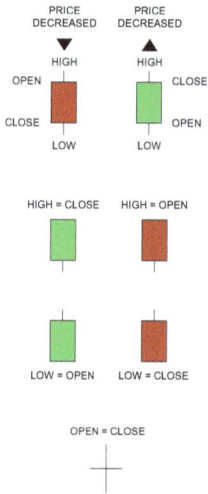

BULLISH REVERSAL PATTERNS

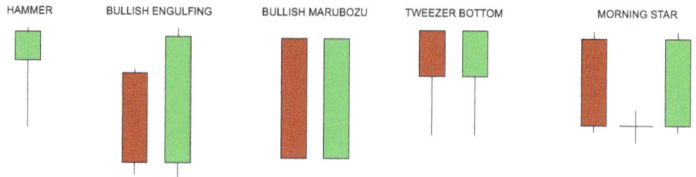

HAMMER   BULLISH ENGULFING   BULLISH MARUBOZU   TWEEZER BOTTOM   MORNING STAR

BULLISH REVERSAL PATTERNS

SHOOTING STAR   BEARISH ENGULFING   BEARISH MARUBOZU   TWEEZER TOP   EVENING STAR

STENGTH OF CANDLESTICKS

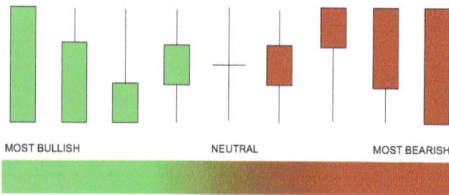

MOST BULLISH   NEUTRAL   MOST BEARISH

INDECISION PATTERNS

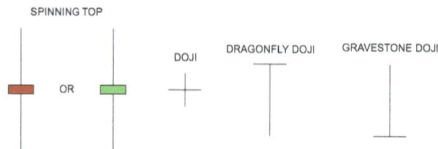

SPINNING TOP

OR

DOJI   DRAGONFLY DOJI   GRAVESTONE DOJI

TRIPPLE BULLISH PATTERNS

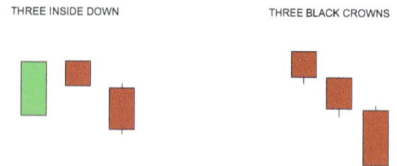

THREE INSIDE UP   THREE WHITE SOLDIERS

TRIPPLE BULLISH PATTERNS

THREE INSIDE DOWN   THREE BLACK CROWNS

Understanding **support and resistance** will allow you to have an idea at what extent the stock will go up or down in a certain timeframe.

Support: Stock price struggles to go below that in certain time frame.

Resistance: Stock price struggles to cross that price.

(Think: It's like a "range" of price that it goes up/down in.)

Remember: If a stock clearly breaks the resistance, that becomes the **new support** and there will be **new resistance**.

Video Module

Risk Vs Reward

This chapter requires knowledge of **"Support/Resistance"** if you skipped that. *Go back and read it in the previous chapter.*

Imagine if you know the probability of your win or loss. Would you get into a trade that has more risk of losing vs winning? *No right?* That's what we are going to learn.

Like I said, " Support and Resistance" are like a range of price that stock moves in. We are going to that knowledge and convert it into something called "RISK AND REWARD"

Stock is all about probability. When going into a trade, you always have some risk and reward. Using support and resistance, we can get an idea of that probability.

Let's get on the video lesson

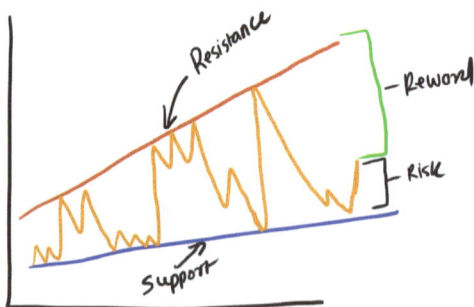

20 Trendlines : Your "Friend"

Repeat after me:

TREND IS MY FRIEND!

The trend is the direction stock price is on in a given timeframe. It will give you an overall idea about what the stock could do in the future. *For example*, $AAPL 's trend is positive since its existence, it tells you that you should ignore day-to-day fluctuation. However, if you find a stock that's doing well today but the overall trend is down, then I would not hold that stock too long, I could daytrade or swing trade, but I will not hold it, as a long-term investment.

In the video:

- Creating trendlines
- How to read trendlines

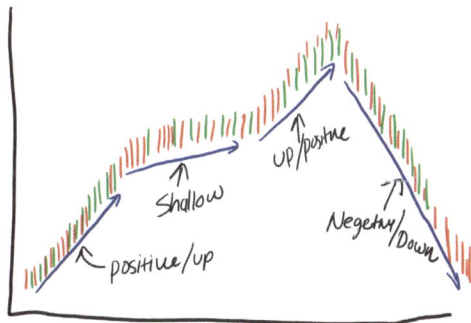

Video Module

Pricing Channel

Pricing channel is just a fancy term for RISK and REWARD (i just created that term, just to make it easier on you). However, the pricing channel is the "channel" that price is moving in and we can craft a pricing channel to see if it will break the support/resistance.

3 Different kinds of pricing channels.

In the video:

- Creating Pricing Channel
- Breaking Point

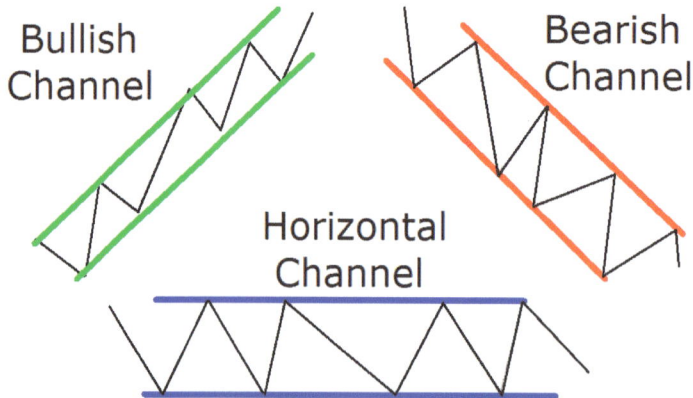

Bullish Channel

Bearish Channel

Horizontal Channel

Video Module

Relative Strength Index, just tells you how hyped up the price is at that given time frame. If price is too hyped up, it's going to go down (Sell Signal) and if RSI is very low, it's bound to go up. RSI tells you if price is a "good deal".

Using RSI, we can decide if it's the right time to take the position. We can combine time frame and RSI to exactly see if taking a position right now is going to have more reward or risk.

(Remember when you bought a stock because a friend of yours posted an Instagram story?, You bought it too and it crashed the next day?... If only you had checked RSI.)

In the video:

- Adding RSI on TradingView
- Using RSI and TimeFrame
- Position Sizing using RSI

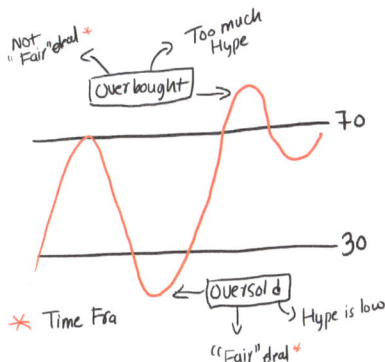

Video Module

Moving Average Convergence Divergence (MACD) or I even call it *"McDonald Indicator"* tells you the momentum the stock price is in. This will help you decide when to take/exit a position. It also tells you if you should wait a little longer so you sell for lower loss. (Yes, sometimes you have to sell for loss and knowing how to take less loss is also a part that makes you a better trader)

In the video:

- Creating MACD
- Interpreting MACD

Video Module

24 Moving Averages

Moving average tells you which direction and price is the stock moving toward. Like the name says, it's an average (mean) of the last 10 prices. Using that information, a line graph is created to show you when you should enter or exit the trades.

There are various types of moving averages: Simple Moving Averages (SMA), Exponential Moving average (EMA). We will focus just on SMA. That's all you need for now.

In the video:

- What is moving averages
- Creating SMA on Trading View
- When to enter/exit & Confirmations

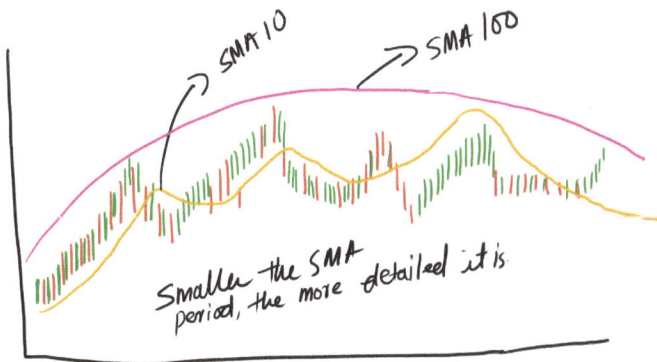

SMA 10

SMA 100

Smaller the SMA period, the more detailed it is

Video Module

People buy and sell a stock because one of two reasons: **Greed or Fear.** So whenever you see someone buying a stock, they might be buying because they want to sell for higher or fear of missing out. Either way, Buy/Sell occurs because of one of those two human behaviors.

Chart Patterns are the result of that human behavior.

In the video:

- Are chart patterns legit?
- How to use CP to trade

Kardashian Butt pattern AKA "Double Bottom"

Video Module

Most Popular Chart Patterns

1. **Broadening Bottoms**

2. **Broadening Formations, Right- Angled and Ascending**

3. **Broadening Formations, Right- Angled and Descending**

4. **Broadening Tops**

5. **Broadening Wedges, Ascending**

6. **Broadening Wedges, Descending**

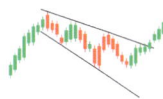

7. **Bump-and-Run Reversal Bottoms**

8. **Bump-and-Run Reversal Tops**

9. **Cup with Handle**

10. **Cup with Handle, Inverted**

Chart Patterns Index

11. Dead-Cat Bounce

12. Dead-Cat Bounce, Inverted

13. Diamond Bottoms

14. Diamond Tops

15. Double Bottoms, Adam & Adam

16. Double Bottoms, Adam & Eve

17. Double Bottoms, Eve & Adam

18. Double Bottoms, Eve & Eve

19. Double Tops, Adam & Adam

20. Double Tops, Adam & Eve

21. Double Tops, Eve & Adam

22. Double Tops, Eve & Eve

Chart Patterns Index

23. Flags

24. Flags, High and Tight

25. Gaps

26. Head-and-Shoulders Bottoms

27. Head-and-Shoulders Bottoms, Complex

28. Head-and-Shoulders Tops

29. Head-and-Shoulders Tops Complex

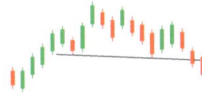

30. Horn Bottoms

31. Horn Tops

32. Island Reversals, Bottoms

33. Island Reversals, Tops

34. Islands, Long

35. Measured Move Down

36. Measured Move Up

37. One-Day Reversals, Bottoms

38. One-Day Reversals, Tops

39. Pennants

40. Pipe Bottoms

41. Pipe Tops

42. Rectangle Bottoms

43. Rectangle Tops

44. Rounding Bottoms

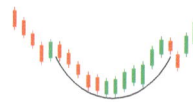

45. Rounding Tops

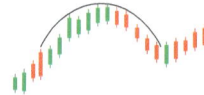

46. Scallops, Ascending

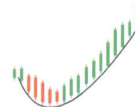

Chart Patterns Index

47. Scallops, Ascending and Inverted

48. Scallops, Descending

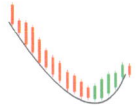

49. Scallops, Descending and Inverted

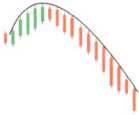

50. Shark

51. Three Falling Peaks

52. Three Rising Valleys

53. Triangles, Ascending

54. Triangles, Descending

55. Triangles, Symmetrical

56. Triple Bottoms

57. Triple Tops

58. Wedges, Falling

59. Wedges, Rising

61. Weekly Reversals, Upside

60. Weekly Reversals, Downside

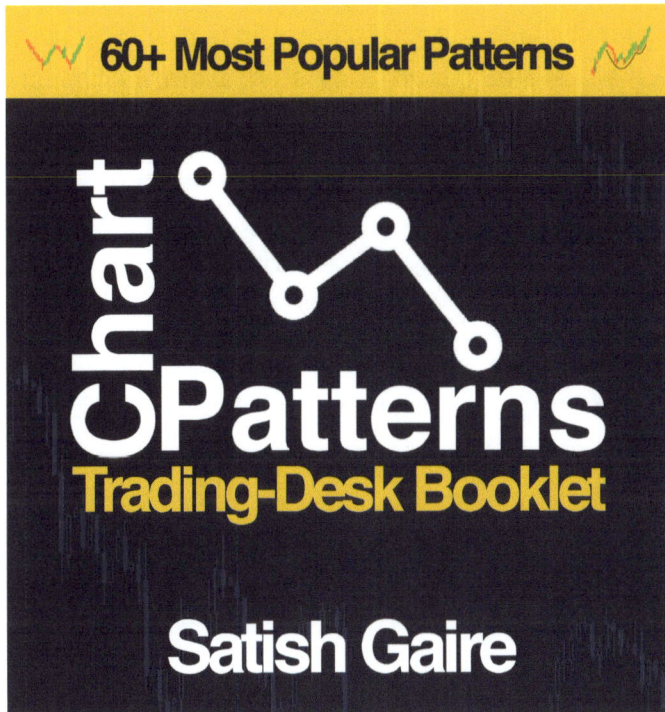

60+ Most Popular Patterns

Chart Patterns

Trading-Desk Booklet

Satish Gaire

Available On

amazon.com   Walmart   BARNES&NOBLE

Fibonacci retracement levels are horizontal lines that indicate where support and resistance are likely to occur. They stem from Fibonacci's sequence, a mathematical formula that originated in the 13th century.

Each level is associated with a percentage. The percentage is how much of a prior move the price has retraced. The Fibonacci retracement levels are 23.6%, 38.2%, 61.8%, and 78.6%. While not officially a Fibonacci ratio, 50% is also used.

The indicator is useful because it can be drawn between any two significant price points, such as a high and a low. The indicator will then create the levels between those two points.

In the video:

- Drawing Fibonacci Retracements
- How To Use It

Video Module

Analyst Price Targets

You know how experts "know" price targets and they know where the stock is headed. Analyst use special tools, research & sometimes insider information to predict what might happen to that stock in the future.

For example, $AAPL might have had a rough year, but its 5 year out look might be good so, Analysts might recommend holding & buying.

Take Analyst recommendations & targets with a grain of salt because they are just predictions and don't mean they are correct every single time. Use this to gauge people's outlook on security.

In the video:

- Where to find Analyst Targets
- How To Use It

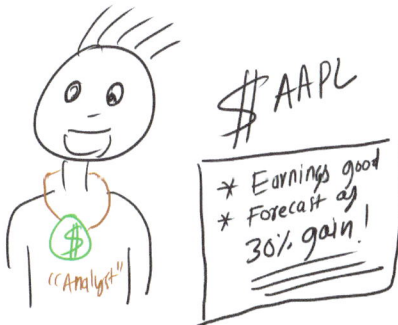

Video Module

28 Taking/Exiting A Position

I gave a stock tip to a friend of mine, he bought it then he sent me a screen-shot of the "profits" he had made, a few days later, when I called him up. He said that it says negative amount.

I asked, "did you not sell it?" He said "you never taught me how to sell"

It's SUPER vital we know how to BUY and ACTUALLY sell. Until you have sold your position, you have neither lost or gained money. A lot of people don't sell their loses for years and then sell it when stock goes up after 2 years, they did not lose money. And some never sell, thus, they have only "gained" in the paper. We have term for this: (Realized Gain/Loss)

In the video:

- Robinhood taking/exiting positon
- ThinkOrSwim taking/existing position
- WeBull taking/exiting position
- Other Platforms

Quantiy +500

Buy   Sell

Video Module

Trading Using Indicators

There are hundreds of indicators that you can use to trade, but I strongly believe that if you focus on mastering the following indicators, you will be ok.

Trading Using RSI

Use the RSI by using the 30 and 70 levels in the oscillator as **oversold** and **overbought** levels respectively. This means that when RSI falls below 30, you aim to buy the financial security that has been sold too much and when the RSI reaches over 70, you aim to sell the financial asset that has been bought too much.

In the video:

- Entry with RSI
- Exit with RSI
- Support & Resistance with RSI

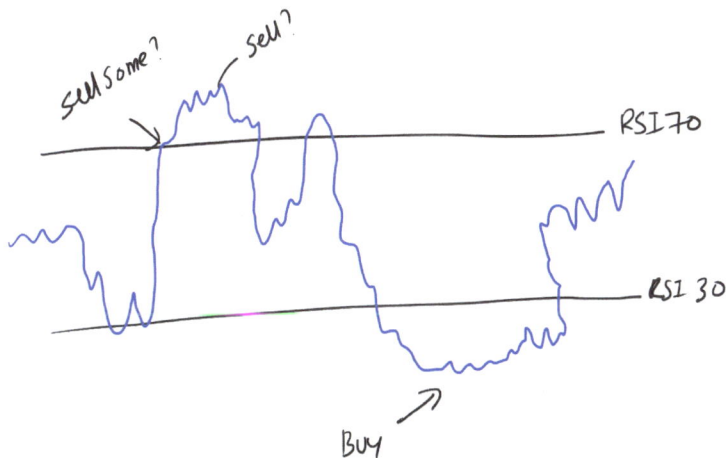

Video Module

Moving average convergence/divergence (MACD) allows you . It is designed to reveal changes in the strength, direction, momentum, and duration of a trend in a stock's price.

With this indicator, we can see which direction is the stock price moving at which rate, so you can decide if you want to buy or sell.

In the Video:

- Using MACD to Trade

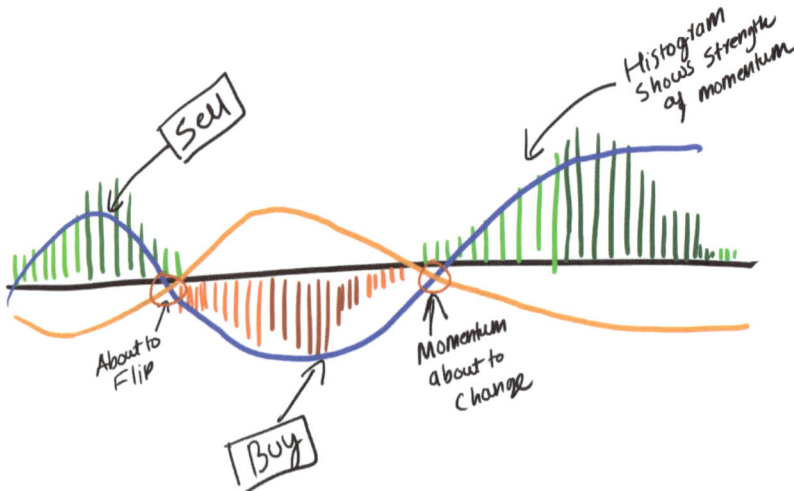

Video Module

A **simple moving average** allows you to see where the price is going and if the current price is above or below the average of a specific period. When asset prices cross over their moving averages, it may generate a trading signal for technical traders.

Buy **when the moving average slopes upward and the closing price crosses above the moving average**. Close the position (sell) when the price closes below the moving average. Sell short when the moving average slopes downward and the closing price crosses below the moving average.

In the video:

- Confirmation & Validation
- Entry and Exit Points
- Using EMA to Trade

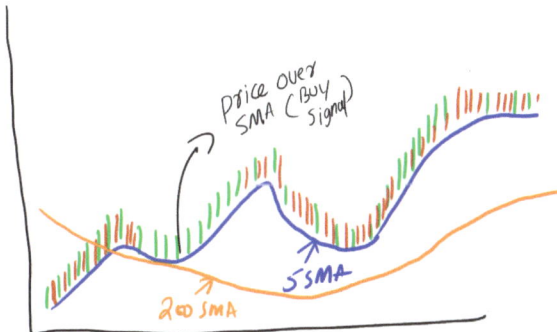

Video Module

32 High Probability & Other Indicators

High Probability just means being able to use more than one Indicator & other external information to make sure that the trade you're about to place has the odd in your favor.

Other Indicators: YES, There are other indicators as well that you can use while trading, but I truly believe that having too many indicators just confuses you, but I want an open line of communication.

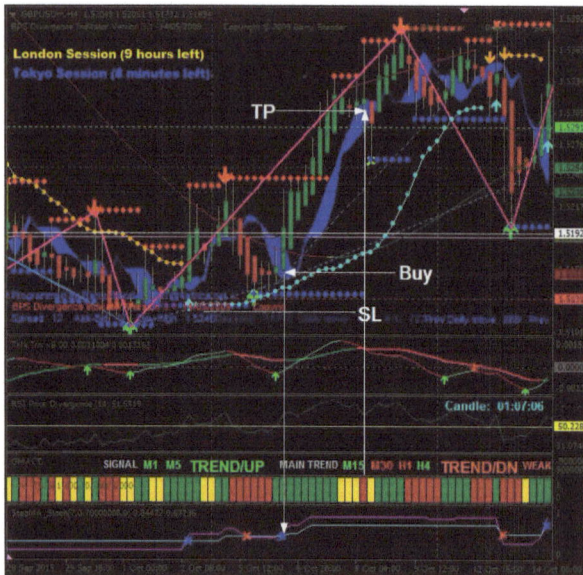

SCAN The QR Code To Learn About Other Indicators and How To Use Them.

Secret Unique
Code: 00195345

Video Module

Company Fundamentals

Most "Day Trading Gurus" will have you skip learning about the company's metrics, but it's important to analyze the health and stability of assets that you are about to invest in.

33 Researching Company

Being able to do **analysis on a company's information and its finances** will allow you to become a better trader. This will allow you to know if this is a *"WAM BAM THANK YOU MA'AM"* kind of stock or it's a keeper.

In the video module, We will find a random company that I have never looked at and I will let you inside my brain on what I am thinking and how I go about using all the things we have learned so far to predict what's the future, what's the risk of investing with this company.

In the video:

- Step by step on researching company
- Looking at history
- SEC : Edgar Database

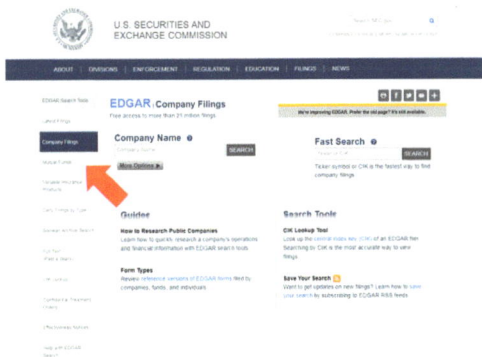

Video Module

34 Metrics and What they mean

Name	What It Means
Market Cap	The number of shares that's available for trading x the current price.
Earnings Per Share (EPS)	EPS indicates how much money a company makes for each share of its stock.
Price To Earnings (P/E)	The P/E ratio shows what the market is willing to pay today for a stock based on its past or future earnings.
Price To Book (P/B)	Shows the value given by the market for each dollar of the company's net worth
Stock Last Price	What was the stock last traded for?
Average Volume	Volume measures the number of shares traded. High volume increasing ovetime is considered "healthy"
Float	Shares that can be traded. Doesn't include shares held by "insiders"
Short Float	The number of shares short-sellers have borrowed from the float. These people expect the stock to crash so they can buy back for cheaper.
Shares Outstanding	The total number of stocks that the company has issued.

We will discuss all these on the video module into detail.

Video Module

Finding Stocks To Play

This is the most "fun" part of the book. After reading these chapters, you will not have to wonder *"what should I trade today?"*, you will have various options and only trade where the probability of REWARD is HIGHER than the RISK.

Volume Trades

Volume trades are trades where we trade the MOST traded stock for that day. This is typically for a quick day trade, In volume trades, the price moves very fast, so you have to decide what point you want to enter and exit before the trade.

These stocks are typically "crappy" companies and you should not be a "bag holder" by not selling. Even if you are loss, it's best to sell them off.

In the video:

- Finding volume trade for that day
- Strategy for volume trade

Ticker	Last	Change	Volume	Signal
ISIG	19.11	84.10%	67634103	Top Gainers
EFOI	3.32	70.26%	194035852	Top Gainers
PPSI	10.79	34.04%	35669432	Top Gainers
DWACW	21.50	30.46%	3556449	Top Gainers
BKKT	17.14	29.75%	19929968	Top Gainers
DWAC	65.42	28.10%	27548923	Top Gainers
PLAB	17.91	25.95%	4437829	New High
JWEL	16.84	12.79%	489051	New High
PLIN	2.89	12.89%	1243120	New High
UNFI	55.61	13.21%	2597797	New High
CFVI	14.99	14.25%	30733775	Overbought
CFVIU	16.23	15.27%	135353	Overbought
EFOI	3.32	70.26%	194035852	Unusual Volume
LEXX	5.60	13.82%	13175357	Unusual Volume
NVEI	57.97	-40.45%	17895389	Unusual Volume
VGII	9.86	0.41%	9176833	Unusual Volume
ESTC	128.31	10.19%	3090867	Upgrades
ALOT	15.76	-7.35%	20595	Earnings Before
AMRS	6.62	8.70%	7172238	Insider Buying

Video Module

Over Reaction Stocks

Overreaction stocks, as the name says, are when people panic about something that's not really something to be worried about.

For Example: Let's say news comes out saying that Tim Cook, CEO of Apple has COVID. People start selling stock. Let's say the price goes down by $20. This is an OVERREACTION. CEO getting COVID is not going to harm the company in long term.

Yes, people might be selling to avoid the loss because they know others will be selling too, but this is a great time to either lower your average or take a position because the rebound happens really quick and you can make money very fast on STABLE companies.

In the video:

- Finding over reaction stocks
- News & Catalyst
- How to play overreactions

Video Module

Insider Trading

Insider trading is illegal when YOU steal the information or use it from first-hand sources to trade, it's not illegal if you find that information in public.

In this lesson, we will learn how to snoop SEC (government's public data-base) and see what companies are planning, see what politicians are buying/selling, and use that to our advantage.

In the video:

- What is insider trading
- 3 Types of ways to find information

Latest Insider Trading | Top Insider Trading Recent Week | Top 10% Owner Trading Recent Week

Filter [All Transactions ▾]

Ticker	Owner	Relationship	Date	Transaction	Cost	#Shares	Value ($)	#Shares Total	SEC Form 4
AMRK	BENJAMIN JEFFREY D	Director	Dec 07	Option Exercise	3.34	5,000	16,700	501,219	Dec 08 07:55 PM
AMRK	BENJAMIN JEFFREY D	Director	Dec 07	Sale	64.71	5,000	323,543	496,219	Dec 08 07:55 PM
AMRS	MCCANN JAMES F	Director	Dec 06	Buy	5.71	17,400	99,354	29,831	Dec 08 07:51 PM
KRT	Cheng Marvin	VP-Manufacturing, Secy & Dir.	Dec 07	Sale	21.52	2,645	56,920	7,325,258	Dec 08 07:41 PM
SPLP	HOWARD JACK L	President	Dec 06	Buy	37.09	16,000	593,442	1,547,152	Dec 08 07:37 PM
ATH	Golden John Leonard	EVP and General Counsel	Dec 07	Sale	81.98	1,875	153,712	39,179	Dec 08 07:34 PM
VRSK	Stephenson Scott G	CEO and President	Dec 08	Option Exercise	61.14	57,920	3,541,229	747,331	Dec 08 07:31 PM
VRSK	Stephenson Scott G	CEO and President	Dec 06	Option Exercise	61.14	73,195	4,475,142	747,331	Dec 08 07:31 PM
VRSK	Stephenson Scott G	CEO and President	Dec 06	Sale	222.12	65,660	14,584,619	689,411	Dec 08 07:31 PM
VRSK	Stephenson Scott G	CEO and President	Dec 08	Sale	226.20	57,920	13,101,287	689,411	Dec 08 07:31 PM
USIO	LONG MICHAEL R	Director	Dec 06	Sale	5.60	2,000	11,200	1,903,873	Dec 08 07:24 PM
USIO	LONG MICHAEL R	Director	Dec 07	Sale	5.55	2,000	11,100	1,901,873	Dec 08 07:24 PM
ID	RIGAUD EDWIN	Director	Dec 06	Buy	2.12	56,450	119,533	227,605	Dec 08 07:23 PM
GDYN	Klimoff Stan	Chief Strategy Officer	Dec 06	Sale	37.24	4,000	148,970	170,639	Dec 08 07:23 PM
GDYN	Klimoff Stan	Chief Strategy Officer	Dec 06	Sale	37.19	3,000	111,572	78,084	Dec 08 07:23 PM
RH	Bottin John P	CEO	Dec 06	Option Exercise	15.03	6,500	103,550	68,941	Dec 08 07:20 PM

Video Module

38 Momentum Stocks

Momentum stocks are stocks that are on the rise, you will enter when the stock is actually moving up, in the middle of it. For these trades, you look at RSI and MACD and see how much of "runway" I got to ride this and you exit the trade before it crashes.

Think of these stocks like *"surfing"* on the ocean waves. Goal is to ride it as much as possible and get out before wave disappears.

In the video:

- Looking at momentum stocks
- When to enter/exist
- How to find momentum stocks

Video Module

39 ▸ Pre-Market & After Hours

Did you know you can buy stocks a few hours before/after the market opens/ closes? **These hours are called Pre-Market and AfterHour.**

Pre-Market trading occurs at 4 a.m. to 9:30 a.m. EST in US markets, This is like getting access to early bird access into stock before the market opens up officially, but usually, the volume is not that high, so your order may not execute. Pre Market movers also indicates how the security will perform when the market opens.

After Hour trading happens from 4 p.m. to 8 p.m. EST in US markets, this is best if you want to trade news that came after the market close. Keep in mind the orders might not execute due to low volume and you have to use a LIMIT order.

In the video module:

- Pre and Aftermarket
- How to play pre-market
- How to play after hour

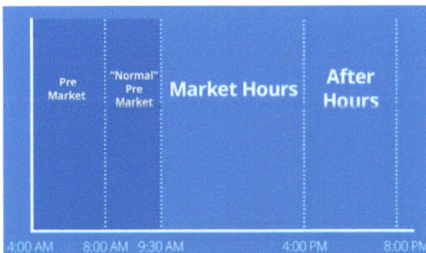

40 Dividends Stocks

Dividend stocks are companies that pay out regular dividends. Dividend stocks are usually well-established companies with a track record of distributing earnings back to shareholders.

These companies want you to hold on to the shares by giving you a small source of income for just owning the stocks. These companies are usually stable and mature.

- Put some of the "Savings" into Dividends Stocks
- Reinvest the Dividends or Withdraw it

In the Video Module:

- Best dividend stocks
- IRA Roth Strategy

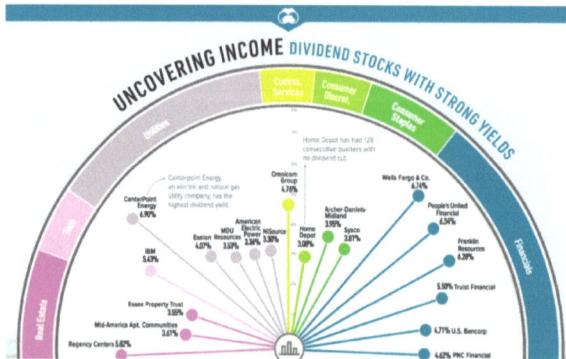

Video Module

Food and Drug Administration (FDA) is in charge of approving any medical ingredients or device that affects humans in the US. Each year, hundreds of companies file for approval and if those companies are listed publicly, we can play FDA approval before it gets approved and if/after it gets approved with different strategies. We will make money regardless if they get approved or not. *Let's watch the video module now.*

FDA Checklist:

[ ] Is stock above $5
[ ] This is not blue-chip/ Mature company
[ ] Is it innovative
[ ] Checked Press Release

In the video:

- What is FDA trades
- Pre-Approval
- Post-Approval

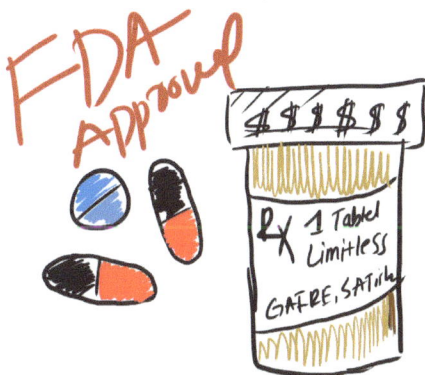

Video Module

Earning Calls

Earning calls are pretty much when companies announce how much money they have made in that quarter. So there will be 4 earning calls each year.

We can play this announcement by either buying stock a few days earlier after looking at their data or playing it on the day of the announcement depending on the "momentum" (see how all the information you learned is getting put together?) Earning calls are usually "Swing Trades".

In the video:

- Finding earning calls calendar
- How to play

Video Module

Public Trending

Wouldn't it be awesome to know which stock people are talking about the most, so you can get in it a little early or even on pre-market before everyone else jumps on? Well, you can!

These are called **Public trending stocks**, stocks that may or may not be financially sound but they are trending, meaning people are talking the most about. Remember, we are never going to fight the market, we are going to get in, make our money and get out. That's it!

In this video:

- Reddit Trending
- Lion Trending
- StockWits
- Twitter

Trending Tickers

These are the top 10 trending streams on Stocktwits right now. Check back every five minutes for updates.

Rank	Symbol	Name	Score	Price	Price % Change
1	IRNT	IronNet Inc	25.43	5.42	↓ 18.19%
2	SOFI	SoFi Technologies Inc	21.98	15.55	↑ 7.27%
3	CALT	Calliditas Therapeutics AB - ADR	20	28.95	↑ 67.26%
4	AMD	Advanced Micro Devices. Inc.	19.38	147.21	↑ 8.52%
5	SPY	SPDR S&P 500	17.67	470.91	↑ 1.63%
6	AMC	AMC Entertainment	17.47	25.58	↑ 4.38%
7	NIO	NIO Inc.	17.42	31.30	↓ 3.02%
8	PLUG	Plug Power Inc.	16.46	32.89	↑ 7.53%
9	SHOP	Shopify	15.31	1379.15	↑ 1.83%
10	CINU·X	Cheems Inu	15.14	---	---

Video Module

44 IPOs

Learning how to play IPO **(Initial public offering)** just adds another source of income via Stocks. It's vital you learn how to play these. If you can get into an IPO at the right time, and sell when its rallying up, you can make hefty profit. Always be on the lookout for new IPOs.

IPO: When a company goes public for the first time.

In the video:

- How to find IPOs
- How to evaluate IPOs
- Looking At IPO SEC doc

Notes:

- IPO stocks fall in about 90 days because the insiders are locked in and are not allowed to sell the stock until 90 days, be ready for this.

Video Module

45   SPAC

Special Purpose Acquisition Company (SPAC) is a new way for companies to go public without actually having revenue and the foundation. Pretty much, it's a "FUND" collected from the public (us) and Institutions to BUY an existing company. So when you invest in " Health SPAC", you know they will buy something in the health industry but don't know what.

In short, SPACs are Shell companies and blank checks. The SPAC owner company decides what to invest in and how to use the funds.

In the video:

- Explaining SPACs
- King Of SPAC- Chamath
- What to look for in SPAC

LISTED SPAC

Cash Held in Trust

Blind pool of cash raised by financial sponsor through IPO to acquire a private operating company

Acquisition typically within 24 months

TARGET COMPANY

Target Operating Company

Fully operating private company

LISTED 'SUCCESSOR' COMPANY

Publicly Listed Operating Company

Value generation through highly incentivized management structure

Video Module

OTC and Penny Stock

Over The Counter (OTC) stocks like the name says, are "shitty" stocks, but that doesn't means that you cannot make money from them. They are usually priced very very low, sometimes fraction of a penny, which means you can buy more units, and when they go up or even decide to get listed on bigger stock exchange like NASDAQ. That's when we hit a jackpot!

OTC are VERY RISKY, but if you know how to play them. You could make a fortune.

In the video:

- How to find OTC Stock
- How to Evaluate OTC

Over-The-Counter Shares

Video Module

Blue Chips

Blue Chip companies are companies that you have heard of, like Apple, Microsoft, AMD, J&J. These companies are household names. They are stable companies that have been proven over time that they can handle it all.

In the video:

- Types of blue chips
- How to invest
- Trendlines

Just FYI - Tesla is not a blue-chip. No matter what you argue. I will prove this to you later when we look at metrics.

Examples:

- ☑ Industry Leader
- ☑ Dependable Business Model
- ☑ A Proven Track Record
- ☑ A history of delivering strong return over the long term
- ☑ Pays Dividends To Shareholders
- ☑ Regular Increase In Payouts

Video Module

48 OverHype: Marijuana/5G/EV

OverHype sectors are pretty much "shiny stocks" that claim to have disrupted an existing industry or something brand new that has no stable history of yet.

These kinds of stock should not be held for too long unless you're sure that this has a good positive long-term outlook (most don't). On these kinds of stock, there is usually a hype for a few months and it dries down, idea is to catch it early enough. These are bubbles that pops sooner or later.

These sectors include: Marijuana, 5G, EV, Space, Blockchain, Crypto etc

In The Video Module:

- Overhype sectors
- How to play them

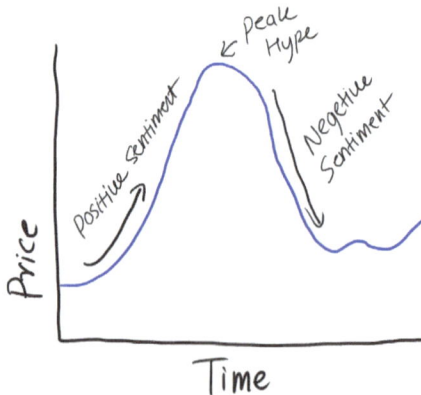

Video Module

WallStreet Bets

"WallStreet Bets" is a forum on a website called *Reddit*. This forum has millions of participants who discuss securities. They also do co-ordinate buying and selling. Joining and lurking on WSB is helpful to see what's coming next & become a part of it.

Remember the $AMC & $GME in 2021? It was caused by them.

Think of it like this, Big banks & institutions play with big money. They can manipulate the market however they wish. WSB is pretty much like an institution for us "retail traders" (little people).

In The Video Module:

- Using WSB Reddit
- WSB Lingo

Video Module

50 Scanner Setup

So far I have given you straight up ways to find stocks to trade, but as you become experienced, it's important for you to learn to use a stock scanner based on #s & technical aspects.

In the video module, I will show you step by step on how to do this. I got you! *(Can I get a follow on my ig? @sgaire)*

In The Video Module:

- FinViz Scanner
- TradingUniversity Scanner
- ThinkOrSwim Scanner

Video Module

Get Daily Stock Alerts & Tools At

StockAlert101.com

StockAlert101 is a online tool that gives you alerts for Stocks, FDA deals and Special IPOS.

Psychology

Most people lose money on stocks because they suck at taking or cutting losses. In the following chapters, we will learn how to master that.

Taking Profits

People suck at taking profits. They see that they have made money on their trade, and then they get greedy and want more. *Until you sell, you have not made "Realized Gains".*

Two ways to take profits:

Target Profit: Before you execute a trade, know the % (percent) gain you want & once you achieve it, you sell, no matter what.

Position Sizing: You sell 50% of the units, then another 25%, and Then Another.

Yes, The stocks could go higher after you sell for profit, but stop losing sleep over it. That's what you want, you want to end up making money on each trade. You are not married to the stock, let it go up/down whatever after you sell.

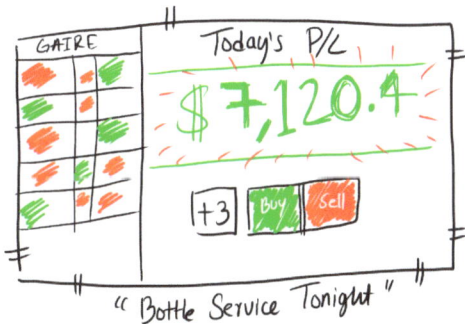

Video Module

Cutting Loss

Cutting loss is when you know you can no longer recover or want to get rid of the stock owned (close position) with a net of a loss.

Understand that you are not really at a loss UNTIL you SELL. "Realized Loss"

When should you cut your loss?

- Don't cut loss when the ENTIRE market is "RED" bleeding
- Free up cash for something else that will bring a return
- OTC & Chinese stocks: Most of these stocks will not rebound
- Can't sleep at night: If this is happening, sell it. Take the loss.

OK. If you have a huge loss and are thinking of doing something "stupid". ***Don't bother. It's not worth it. Delete that brokerage app and get a job & go to gym.***

Video Module

53 ❯ To Average Up or Down

After you buy a security, It could go up or down, then you have a choice if you should buy more at a higher price because you think it will go higher or buy more at a lower price because you think it will bounce off or this is the "new dip". In most cases, it's best not to average down or up because the temporary price doesn't indicate what's going to happen.

When To Average Down:

- Price fell due to "over-reaction"
- Company Fundamentals same
- Long Term Investment Horizon

When To Average Up:

- To Catch Rising Momentum
- Bought Too little shares initially on growing stock
- Blue Chip Companies

In Video Modules:

- Averaging Up or Down
- Possible Risks

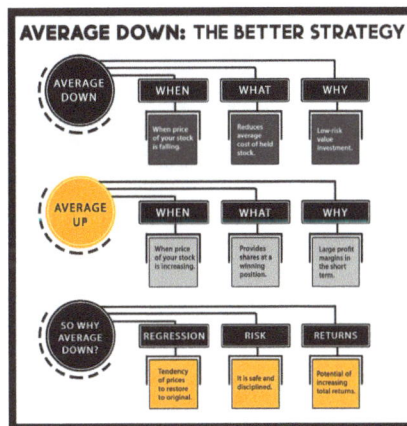

AVERAGE DOWN: THE BETTER STRATEGY

Video Module

Putting it all Together

Now we put everything we have learned into one big process. Eventually, they will all come naturally to you. *You are almost there!*

54 Setup Alerts and Watchlist

Before you start trading, It's important to have some sort of watchlist based on what you like to trade, it could be weed stocks or tech. These could also be the scanned stocks that you learned how to do in an earlier chapter.

Your brokerage probably has a watchlist/alert but I think Yahoo Watchlist is probably better because of its unique features.

You need to know how a certain stock performs throughout the day to really understand it. It will give you leverage to know when to trade. *For example*, some stocks do really back during power hour (1 hr before closing) some do really well.

In The Video Module:

- Setting up Alerts
- Best Way To Create Watchlist

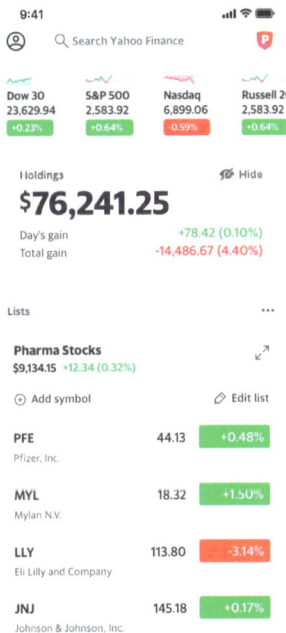

Ultimate Trading Plan

Finally, We are ready! Scan the QR code & Get on the Video Module & we will apply everything you have learned on one go!

For Each Trade, You will go through this, step by step!

- [ ] Choose A Time Frame (Daytrade, Swing, Long Term)
- [ ] Do you have a higher Reward Vs Risk? (Support & Resistance)
- [ ] Confirmation? (Moving Average)
- [ ] Is this a Good Deal? (RSI)
- [ ] Trading Above Long-Term SMA?
- [ ] Directional Strength Ok? (MACD)
- [ ] Any Upcoming Catalyst/ News?
- [ ] What is Analyst Target?
- [ ] Are There Other Stocks Better Probability?
- [ ] Long Term Outlook?
- [ ] How much am I investing? (Position Sizing)
- [ ] How much is my target?
- [ ] When do I cut loss?
- [ ] Execute

Video Module

Advance

The following chapters will help you understand some concepts in stock market to help you become a better trader.

Sheep Feeds
and Feeding
in Western Canada

Steve Mason, PhD

later, Provincial Livestock Nutritionist.

Many thanks to Dale Engstrom, Wray Whitmore and Glenna McGregor for their inva
comments and suggestions for improvement of the text.

Attributable image credits:

Cover image: licensed iStock photo; Figure 1.1: licensed Alamy stock photo; Figures 1
and 1.9: Norman Criddle in G.H. Clark and M.O. Malte, Fodder and Pasture Plants, C
Department of Agriculture, 1923; Figure 3.7: Penn State University; Figure 6.1, Condi
Scoring Reference, p. 62 and Figure 6.14: UK Agriculture and Horticulture Developm
2019; Figure 6.6: Canada Plan Service; Figure 6.7; Midwest Plan Service; Figure 6.9: M
Cooper and D.W. Morris, Grass Farming, Farming Press Ltd., 1973.

About the author:

Steve Mason obtained both his B.Sc. (Biochemistry) and Ph.D. (Animal Science) from the University of British Columbia. Following a post-doctoral fellowship in medical pharmacology at the University of Calgary, he became a sheep farmer for several years which led to stints as Provincial Sheep Specialist and later, Provincial Livestock Nutritionist, with the British Columbia Ministry of Agriculture.

Moving back to Alberta, Steve became Manager of ProLivestock Nutrition/Management Specialists, a consulting unit of United Grain Growers, later Agricore United. Subsequently, after a short assignment as Senior Extension Associate with Cornell University's Pro-Dairy program, Steve established AgroMedia International Inc., a business that provides knowledge translation and transfer services as well as contract scientific and technical support to the Canadian livestock industries. Oper under the name 'AgInformatics' the company also provides data management and an services to the agricultural research community. More recently, a partnership operati 'Farm Animal Care Associates' has focused on assisting livestock producers with the of best management practices for animal health and welfare. Since 2010, Steve has ser an Adjunct Associate Professor with the University of Calgary Faculty of Veterinary N teaching nutrition, mentoring graduate students and participating in research. He is a Professional Animal Scientist and a Diplomate of the American College of Animal N

Disclaimer:

56   ETFs

An exchange-traded fund (ETF) is a type of security that tracks an index, sector, commodity, or another asset. They are pretty much "better version of Mutual Funds"

You can use ETFs to hedge, for retirement accounts like IRA, to judge market sentiment and even trade them like a normal stock but with lower risk since they are "weighted indexes", meaning, they contain more than 1 company. For example, A tech ETF might contain FB, Google, Amazon, TSLA etc. If one of these companies underperforms, it might not affect ETF as much depending on how much weight (%) is on ETF.

In Video Module:

- ETFs Tracking
- How To Use Them

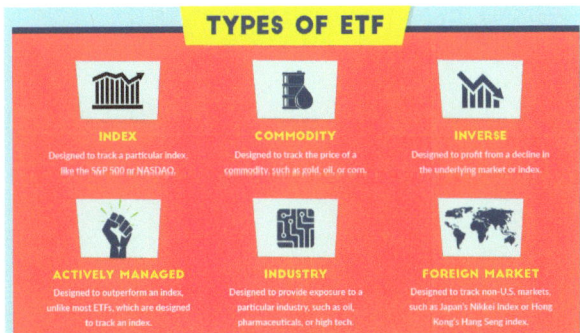

Video Module

Stock Splits

There are 2 types of stock splits **a forward split and a reverse split**. A forward split is when a company increases the number of outstanding shares held by current shareholders.

Forward Splits: They give you more stocks than you own. For example, if they do 2 for 1, they give you 2 stocks for having 1. Normally, they do this to make stock affordable and raise money.

Reverse Splits: If you own 10 units, and they do 1 for 10, then they will reduce your 10 stocks to 1 stock, they usually do this to prevent delisting from the exchange or make it look like they are strong.

	Pre-Split	Post-Split
2-for-1		
# of Shares	10M	20M
Shares Price	$10	$5
Market Cap	$100M	$100M
3-for-1		
# of Shares	10M	30M
Shares Price	$10	$3.33
Market Cap	$100M	$100M
3-for-2		
# of Shares	10M	15M
Shares Price	$10	$6.66
Market Cap	$100M	$100M
Reverse Split		
1-for-10		
# of Shares	10M	1M
Shares Price	$1	$10
Market Cap	$10M	$10M

Video Module

Satish Gaire

58 Level 2 Data

Level 2 data is an optional feature that a lot of brokerage offer, usually free but you may need to enable it from your account setting or ask them for it.

Think of Level 2 data is a "Book" of orders. You can see where people are waiting to buy, where people want to sell, the sizes of the orders. This will help you make better trades because you have an "idea of what to expect".

- Looking at sectors
- Sector vs Specific company correlation
- Choosing where to invest

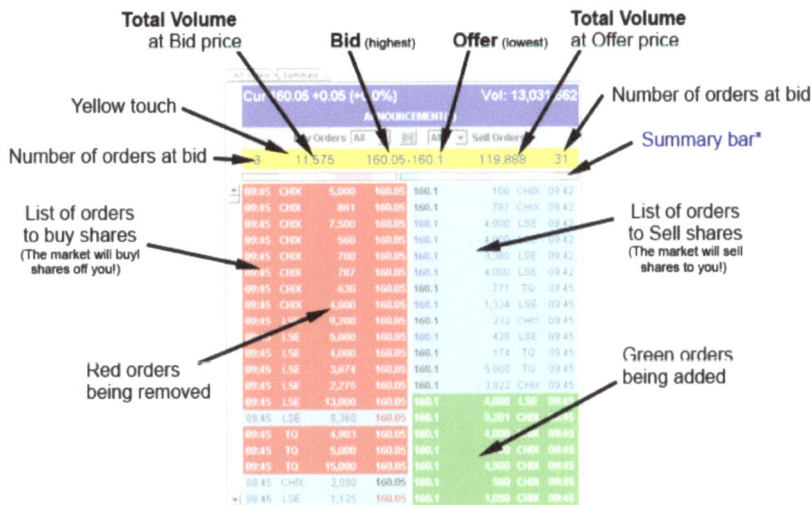

Total Volume at Bid price

Bid (highest)

Offer (lowest)

Total Volume at Offer price

Yellow touch

Number of orders at bid

Number of orders at bid

Summary bar*

List of orders to buy shares (The market will buy! shares off you!)

List of orders to Sell shares (The market will sell shares to you!)

Red orders being removed

Green orders being added

Video Module

59 Further Education

Congratulations! On finishing the book.

If you went through the entire book, you are now among the 1% who actually know how to trade properly instead of just fooling around.

Next: I expect to update video modules as needed, I also encourage you to go to TradingUniversity.io and REGISTER so you can get the updates & Free Courses.

Thank you for making me part of your trading journey. Since my early days, I always wanted to make an impact on people's lives and I hope this book has served that purpose.

Yours Truly,

Satish Gaire

@sgaire

@gairesatish

https://SatishGaire.com

www.ingramcontent.com/pod-product-compliance
Lightning Source LLC
Chambersburg PA
CBHW042058210326
41597CB00045B/68